THE THINGS WE DON'T TALK ABOUT

Our Money Narrative and the Impacts on Our Financial Wellness - Workbook

HEATHER COLEMAN

Lucky Book Publishing

MY GIFT TO YOU

I am so glad you're here!

As my Gift to you, get FREE Access to the Audiobook of Our Money Narrative and other bonus content by scanning the QR Code below or visiting HeatherColeman.ca

INTRODUCTION

Welcome to "Our Money Narrative" Financial Wellness Workbook, a resource designed to help you actively engage with the questions and key takeaways outlined in the accompanying book.

This workbook is crafted to provide you with practical space to complete exercises, reflective prompts, and actionable tools that will empower you to take charge of your financial journey.

Whether you are looking to create financial goals, answer the reflection questions, add your savings goals, or write some jot notes each section is available to reinforce your learning and inspire meaningful changes in your financial habits.

I hope this resource helps you in making the commitment to yourself in applying the insights gained, you'll be better equipped to achieve your financial wellness goals and build a secure and prosperous future.

CHAPTER 1: The History Behind the Story

Questions for you to think about before we get started:

1. Do you have any money stories from your childhood that you recall?

2. Do you have any misconceptions about money that you can name before we get started?

3. Do you have any preconceived notions about your own money narrative?

CHAPTER 2: Money Myths Part 1

Self-Reflection Box 1 page 24

1. How many times have you asked for a raise?

2. How many times have you job-shopped for some extra income?

3. Have you considered getting a side hustle to earn more?

Self-Reflection Box 2 page 26

1. Do you find yourself speaking negatively or positively about your money situation?

2. Do you surround yourself with those who are positive money characters? Or negative?

3. When you are doing a money task – what is your mood? Positive, negative, indifferent?

REFLECTION QUESTIONS WORKSHEET

1. Do you find yourself speaking negatively or positively about your money situation?

2. Do you surround yourself with those who are positive money characters? Or negative?

3. When you are doing a money task – what is your mood? Positive, negative, indifferent?

4. What money myth impacts you?

5. What are you mindful of when it comes to misconceptions about your money?

6. What is your excuse statement? The one you use to justify your spending.

7. Reflect on how the thought of more money impacts your narrative.

CHAPTER 3: Money Myths Part 2

Introduction Reflection Questions:

- Do I find myself using either of them as an excuse?

- Are there any other myths that impact you and your money narrative?

Self-Reflection Question Box Page 38

1. What's your excuse for not getting started with managing your money?

2. Do you think you cannot learn?

3. Any other reason you haven't started?

Where you can make your financial wellness a priority?

1. Instead of scrolling through reels, could you look at your budget for 10 minutes?

2. Can you update your net worth tracker for 15 minutes a month?

3. Can you add in some financial goals for yourself? Realistic ones?

4. What is in your way to make this a priority?

Reflecting on your household:

Was money a sore spot?

Were there arguments about money? Misalignments?

Where did my family fall in that spectrum; am I doing the same things?

Reflection Question Box Page 43

Do you know what is blocking you?

Is it time?

Is it an emotional reaction?

Is it feeling inadequate?

Do you feel you have it under control?

REFLECTION QUESTIONS WORKSHEET

Myth 3:

1. What's your excuse for not getting started with managing your money?

2. Any other reason you haven't started?

Myth 4:

1. Where can I put the time to commit:

2. What specific task am I committing to:

CHAPTER 4: Why Financial Wellness Matters

Reflection Question Box Page 52

Money Contentions you have in your household

What are they about?

Are there specific themes?

Are there specific stressors?

Reflection Question Box Page 60

Do you find yourself looking at the Canadian Tire magazine for the next sale?

Looking at new cars? Going grocery shopping?

Reflection Question Box Page 63

I want you to pause and reflect on this section to see where the impact of financial wellness is impacting your life.

- Relationship

- Health

- Work

- Others

Reflection Questions:

Areas to rewrite your money narrative

If it is in your relationship, maybe you can start the dialogue about money narratives with your partner. Ask them what theirs is. If they know?

If it is your health being impacted, maybe you can carve out time in your day, week, or month to make your commitment to your overall health by managing your finances. Similar to how people put a "workout" block in the calendar, maybe you can put a financial health block in yours. What is your plan?

When it comes to work, maybe you can discuss with your employer about looking into some financial wellness programming. Does work offer Financial Wellness Support?

Are there any other aspects of your wellness you feel are impacted by your finances?

CHAPTER 5: Where Am I At?

Think to yourself

1. Do I even know where I am?

2. Do I fall into multiple buckets?

3. Am I being honest with my situation?

4. Do I have a plan/strategy to move forward?

Reflection Question Box Page 71

Do you resonate with either of these buckets?

More Reflection Questions page 71

If I am in debt, what is preventing me from paying it off?

- I feel I have other bills that come first

- I continue to overspend every month, and I never have enough to pay the minimum or just above

- I am not sure why. When I think about it, I continue to go out for dinner and buy Amazon Prime products regularly, and the debt sits there

- I have been able to pay it off, but the example of life resonates with me. Life is getting in the way that causes me to slip back into debt. However, when I am not dealing with "life extra stuff" I feel I can manage my debt

If I am living-paycheque-to-paycheque, what is preventing me from preparing for "life curveballs":

- I barely have enough at the end of the month to put away

- Other "things" come up every month that I do not put money away for life events

- I like my lifestyle, and I do not want to put money away for things that do not matter right now

Reflection Questions Page 75

Do I know my investment style?

- Does it accurately reflect the right amount of time I have to invest?

- Does it accurately reflect the risk level I should be considering?

- Do I know the fees I am paying regarding these investments?

  » Management Expense Ratios (MER)

  » Deferred Sales Charges (DSC)

  » Discount Broker Fees

  » Brokerage Commissions

  » Fees for service

  » Trading fees or commissions

  » Sales charges (front-end load/initial)

- Do I understand how these fees impact my returns?

- Am I diversified enough in my portfolio that if something dips, I will be ok?

- Have I considered my investing strategy to include key accounts such as the RRSP/TFSA in Canada?

- Am I utilizing my spousal options, if married?

- Am I aware of all the investing options available to me?

- Have I considered looking into alternatives such as real estate?

- Have I considered self-directed investments?

Reflection Questions Box Page 79

1. Do you earn an income? If Yes, you need a Will.

2. Are you over 18? If Yes, you need a Will.

3. Do you have any assets? If yes, you need a Will.

   a. An asset does not have to be big – but if you have a pet, a car, a dresser in your room – whatever, it is best to plan what you want to happen to those items (precious or not).

List all your assets

REFLECTION QUESTIONS WORKSHEET page 81

1. Which Bucket am I in?

```
┌─────────────────────────────────────────────────┐
│                                                 │
│                                                 │
│                                                 │
│                                                 │
│                                                 │
└─────────────────────────────────────────────────┘
```

2. If I am in debt, what is preventing me from paying it off?

   - I feel I have other bills that come first

   - I continue to overspend every month, and I never have enough to pay the minimum or just above

   - I am not sure why. When I think about it, I continue to go out for dinner and buy Amazon Prime products regularly, and the debt sits there.

   - I have been able to pay it off, but the example of life resonates with me. Life is getting in the way that causes me to slip back into debt. However, when I am not dealing with "life extra stuff," I feel I can manage my debt.

```
┌─────────────────────────────────────────────────┐
│                                                 │
│                                                 │
│                                                 │
│                                                 │
└─────────────────────────────────────────────────┘
```

3. If I am living -paycheque-to-paycheque, what is preventing me from preparing for "life curveballs":

- I barely have enough at the end of the month to put away

- Other "things" come up every month that I do not put money away for life events

- I like my lifestyle, and I do not want to put money away for things that do not matter right now

4. If I am saving/investing, do I know the fees I am paying?

5. Do I have a Will?

6. Am I diversified enough?

CHAPTER 6: What Do I Do Now?

Net Worth Tracking Example

Example of a Net Worth Tracker statement from Enriched Academy's training.

Net Worth Tracking Tips

- Gather all your bank statements, credit card statements, pension information, investment account statements from the previous month

- List all the properties you own

- List all vehicles including recreational (boats, ATCs, etc)

- Do you have any collectibles worth value?

- Gather all your pay stubs or highlight the amount of money that gets deposited into your account each pay

- Gather all your debts/liabilities including personal loans, student loans, credit cards, lines of credits, mortgages etc.

Budgeting Tips

- Gather all your bank statements, credit card statements, pension information, investment account statements for the last three months

- Grab your favourite coloured highlighters (Yellow, Blue, Pink)

- Bring out a calculator to add up the amounts OR use an Excel sheet to help determine averages

- Are there any irregular expenses that do not show up in the three months of statements that you have but know they are coming?

  » Kids sport fees

  » Registration fees

  » Vacations

  » etc?

1. **Think of the 3-5 things that bring you joy in a month.**

2. **Now think about the 3-5 items based on your spending that do not have much meaning.**

Reflection Questions

1. What Budget Tool will I use?

2. Do I find the idea of budgeting an issue for my money narrative?

3. Can I improve my budgeting strategy?

4. Do I net worth track?

5. What tool will I be using to net worth track?

6. When will I start my budget?

7. When will I start net worth tracking?

CHAPTER 7: Understanding It Isn't The Same Playbook For All - and That's Ok

Should I pay off High-Interest Debt and/or Save Money?

Should I be saving for my retirement?

What is my financial goal?

My Pledge to Myself

I will start by

I will measure my success by

I will stay accountable by

My goal for the next six months is

BONUS CHAPTER: Divorce and Money

Do I know my finances?

Do I know my spouse's finances?

What can I afford?

Do I have a support system? Who are they?

What chattels are the most important to me? Why?

What is my price of freedom? What am I ok to compromise on?

Am I emotionally prepared for the separation/divorce?

ABOUT THE AUTHOR

Heather Coleman, Financial Wellness Geek, is a dynamic leader dedicated to fostering financial wellness across varying organizations throughout Canada. She researched the impacts of Financial Wellness on Employees and empowering individuals to make informed financial decisions while she completed her Masters of Business Administration from Thompson Rivers University. The successful completion of her MBA led to presenting her research, in collaboration with Dr. Scott Rankin at the ASAC Conference in 2024.

Leading the growth and development of the Associations and Corporations division at Enriched Academy, Heather actively collaborated with Canadian Companies, guiding them in establishing a robust culture of financial well-being among employees or their respective memberships.

Heather's passion has led her to travel the country engaging thousands of Canadians in breaking the barriers of having real "money talk" without the pressure of having to buy.

"Education is a super power and if we take that mindset to our financial wellness, it is life changing".

Beyond her corporate prowess, Heather is a passionate ringette player, showcasing her commitment to both teamwork and athleticism, and a proud mother of two beautiful girls. Heather's multifaceted approach underscores her commitment to holistic well-being, in the workplace, home and on the ice.

Instagram: @hcoleman8
Website: HeatherColeman.ca

thank you

Thank you for reading my book!

Dear Reader,

You made it! Thank you for walking with me through Our Money Narrative Workbook. Whether you completed every exercise or simply reflected on the stories that shaped your financial life, I hope this workbook gave you space to explore, heal, and reclaim your personal money narrative with honesty and empowerment.

If I could ask a quick favor: if you found this workbook meaningful, would you consider leaving a positive review on Amazon or Goodreads? Your words could help someone else feel less alone in their financial journey and encourage them to begin rewriting their own story. Reviews are one of the most powerful ways to help others find this resource—and to support the mission behind it.

With gratitude,
Heather Coleman

MY GIFT TO YOU

I am so glad you're here!

As my Gift to you, get FREE Access to the Audiobook of Our Money Narrative and other bonus content by scanning the QR Code below or visiting HeatherColeman.ca

www.ingramcontent.com/pod-product-compliance
Lightning Source LLC
Chambersburg PA
CBHW071443210326

41597CB00020B/3928